Homo sapiens: Species Exemplar

Fifteen Classic Essays about Human Intelligence

Dr. Dennis V. Burke

DEDICATION

Dedicated to my family who are present, those who came before, and all people who encourage others to think.

CONTENTS

"Never forget that intelligence rules the world and ignorance carries the burden. Therefore, remove yourself as far as possible from ignorance and seek as far as possible to be intelligent."
—Marcus Garvey

INTRODUCTION

Today Homo sapiens, wise men, exist at the apex of a dynamic and complex food chain on the planet Earth. As the apex predator with multiple intelligence and creative imagination, Homo sapiens possess an innate capacity for survival. From the creative imagination of our species evolved all of the creations that gave us advantages over other living creatures. But, this very capacity brings us to the brink of an unknown future in which every skill we have learned might not be enough to protect us. The idea that Homo sapiens can become extinct seems extreme, however; our species is capable of supreme benevolence and extreme violence. It is men who threaten their own existence.

The history of the planet's four plus billion years reveals mysteries of a long line of Homos who are closely related to modern human and who have disappeared. They are our relatives who are now footnotes in our history. Researchers have recorded the extinction of Homo Heidelbergensis, Homo Rudolfensis, Homo Habilis, Homo Floresiensis, Homo Erectus, and Homo Neanderthalensis. These are only a few of the species which we have found. From the future, the history of Homo sapiens might be simply another chapter in the evolution of a living planet. Unless we develop new habits and alter the trajectory of our impact, Homo sapiens might be replaced by Homo Machina.

In the future of the machine and a species without introspective ability, our brains and emotional intelligence will be meaningless. Our security is at best fragile. In our search to understand self, we find traces of man's presence only for sixty-six million years. In a book of life with four billion pages, the final sixty-six million might be the endnotes. Much about the planet and man are unknown. Consider that without mirrors and reflection, we might be unable to describe the self. No man has seen his brain, and so it is possible that while we search the cosmos and through history, the greatest mystery remains the identity, character, and origin of our species, the brain. Let us journey into the stories of who we might be.

ESSAY 1 INTRODUCTION TO HOMO SAPIENS AND INTELLIGENCE

The brain of Homo sapiens is unquestionably the source and identity of the being. The brain of mankind is the source of our species inherent intelligence, and without this capacity, we would have nothing to build on. Long before the advent of machines, Homo sapiens relied on intelligence to survive. Personal health; physical size, speed, flexibility, knowledge, survival skills, and attitudes, were the primary resources for individual and groups. The group with a better system of communication, more members, and unifying values had greater chances of surviving. The ability to learn and grow; be self-aware, and for reasoning might be the reason we are still here today.

Logically the ability to cooperate in Homo sapiens provided our species with a supreme advantage over others. No single individual would have hunted a mammoth nor could have defended himself and family from predators for prolong periods. The fact that Homo sapiens are the dominant species of today means his kind evolved, and he developed intelligence that set his kind apart. Having shared values that were principle-based would have been the basis for trust and respect. Because of his intelligence and the ability to grow, Homo sapiens position within the eco-system has changed from that of prey to the collective predator.

In Homo sapiens, the capacity for teamwork and group success depended on the ability of the group members to communicate. Before machines, all strategies likely flowed out from man's creative imagination. Where communication and strategic execution failed, people paid the price with their lives. Today our machine aggregate data and make projections; the comfort makes our species soft, less intelligent, and more dependent.

Without the convenience of machines, only a very small percentage of people might survive for a week in the environment of early men. We can imagine that hunger and death were constant reminders that cooperation and teamwork were in the best interest of the tribe. Now our success depends on the capacity of our hard drive and the processing speed of our machines. Without access to satellite and Global Positioning Systems few members of modern society might be able to travel from point "A" to "B" without being confused. Without microwave and frozen food, many people might starve, and without modern medicine, most people would die.

Imagine that should any group of animal agree to cooperate, and if they can work to further a single system, the potential for their success increases. Therefore, the emotional intelligence to subordinate social values to principle-based objectives is crucial for actual success. Social achievements are superficial when they are not built on the foundation of principles. People who have valid and accurate mental maps of their goals develop the attitudes and habits that promote their success. Whenever you visualize yourself as a teacher during the process of learning, your level of engagement with the material is much different than when you see yourself simply as a student.

Early man understood this fact so he learned and taught the skills for survival to his team and offspring because it is the only way he would have been able to promote his survival. The fact that we are here today as the species exemplar and the apex predator means our forerunners made better choices than the competitors they face.

Should our choices be of poorer quality than the choices of earlier man and should our intelligence diminish; nature will produce a species to rule at the apex of the food chain.

Let us begin our journey…

ESSAY 2 BECOMING HOMO MACHINA

The esoteric philosophy of the hundredth monkey and the leap that any group will take when enough of its members learn valid knowledge remains consistent throughout history. The growth and development of Homo sapiens exemplify the relationship between knowledge and growth. Questions about the relationship between the development of our species and the acquisition of knowledge are obscured only by the confusion and semantics of our arguments.

Our species continues to evolve, maybe not in a biological sense; instead, we are becoming one with our machines. As we merge with our machines, we become a much different species from earlier man. In the beginning, as we understand, man lived in caves, maybe in small groups, and survived by foraging. He hunted and fought to survive. He fought the elements, moved constantly, and more than likely, he met a tragic end.

However, after enough members of the different groups learn to domesticate animals instead of simply slaughtering them for food, whenever enough people learned to cultivate crops; man earned the right

4

to stop wandering. The species of man who did not acquire these skills are now extinct. Homo sapiens or wise humans with the new knowledge of farming enabled his collective to transform the lifestyle of their group and by extension species. With the new knowledge, man created communities, metropolis, countries, and federations. Most importantly, when people stayed in any place long enough, they created the time and space in which to learn and share the new wisdom. Today man lives in environments with millions of other people, and he has the expectations that he should live a long and prosperous life.

Because man has created the space and time to think by spending less time focused on surviving against the elements, the rate of his evolution now increases exponentially. Homo sapiens no longer stand guard at the edge of his fortification because he has created societies with rules and enforcers. Out of mans' imagination emerged societies of class where farmers cultivate, doctors practice medicine, and teachers educate. Our national identities are defined by our status as developing countries, third world, or First World. Our brain is the most complex organ in the body, and we know this by the amount of energy it consumes. Therefore, by redirecting more resources to our brain, we are expanding our creative and innovative capacities.

The net result is that today, we are learning and growing at a much faster rate than ever before. We are knowledge workers in the information age. Our species now face a new challenge and an important choice. We now face the decision about whether we choose to grow or do we allow our technologies to guide us into the future.

While scholars of various persuasions, religious, political, and academics, argue about the validity of science, the technocrats have unleashed the evolutionary potentials of our machines. Our machines are working to create the ideas that we have programmed into their designs. The ideas are from our imagination, and their meanings reflect our intentions.

When we rethink the meaning of evolution, what we have become is evidently much different from who we were. Across the landscape where an earlier man walked we now fly, where he hunted in earlier times today we farm, where early man fought with sticks, stones, and then with swords we fight with remote controlled machines, and our microwaves have replaced the need for fire. Where our ancestors wondered among nature we have paved the landscapes and built our cities.

Self-awareness in mankind is the most often touted difference between man and others in the animal kingdom. Likewise, we possess the ability to be mindful and to make ethical choices. Unfortunately, as mankind merges first with the smartphone, then into the World Wide Web, and finally to surrogates and avatars, he will inevitably lose the relationships that make him human. When Homo sapiens are finally divorced from the experiences of social interaction, our species become the machine, and our choices become mechanical.

Today we argue whether global warming is real while the climate changes in front of our eyes, and we witness the extinction of cultures and species. From some time in the future a newer version of man, *Homo Machina*, will look back at this time and note that we were never in charge and that our steady march to becoming machines was inevitable.

We are standing at the edge of an abyss, and the question for us to answer is this, do we jump in or do we simply allow ourselves to fall?

The end.

ESSAY 3 THE EVOLUTION OF GROUP AND IDEAS THROUGH EXEMPLARS

Homo sapiens stand apart from other animals as the species exemplar because they possess creative imagination and multiple intelligences. Out of the creative imagination, our species created the pyramids, farming, printing press, ships, cities, politics, religion, and harnessed energy. Through multiple intelligences, our species continue to learn and push the boundaries of possibilities.

By combining man's imaginative faculty with his multiple intelligences, our species can survive and thrive anywhere within the range from a dependent to an apex predator. How and where man operates within this dynamic continuum of existence is determined only by his choices. One person might choose to function as a contributing member of a group, another might stand apart as an observer, and still, another might prey upon a group and its resources. The role each man chooses might benefit self or suit the needs of a group, and he might decide to follow or lead.

Although the basic biological makeup of Homo sapiens has shared characteristics and genetic markers, the breaks within the evolutionary experience of our species produced changes to the social, geographical, and cultural patterns of different groups. Some of the evolutionary changes were subtle, while others were dramatic. Regardless of the level of changes, the results manifest as climatic preferences, geographical locations, religious practices, language variances, and cultural and attitudinal biases of groups. Each group now amplifies their differences as proof of its superiority above another and the species becomes embroiled in perpetual intergroup conflicts based on sentience.

The core of man's existence revolves around his choices. Sentience is the capacity to perceive and process subjective experiences. Choices are informed by knowledge. Knowledge is the function of values and beliefs. Therefore, our choices evolve out of a constant looping of ideas in our heads. The critical behavior that causes shifts within the thought patterns of Homo sapiens is the ability to impose interruptions in thinking. Any man or woman who can deliberately interrupt sentience will stand apart as a thought leader.

Thought leaders within the species and a group might become the exemplar's exemplar. Abraham, Muhammad, Solomon, Galileo, Confucius, Martin Luther, Genghis Khan, Napoleon Bonaparte, Alexander the Great, Albert Einstein, Stalin, Hitler, Gandhi, Aristotle, Adam Smith, Marie Stopes, Rosa Parks, and Mandela are exemplars at particular times in the human story. The impact of exemplar can be positive or negative. Whether real or fictional, their stories represent unique ideas that diverged from the conventional beliefs of the time and resulted in schools of ideas that remain with us today in at least vestigial forms.

The end.

ESSAY 4 IDEAS THE SEEDS OF HUMANITY

Ideas are the most powerful creations to emerge from the human mind. The power of an idea is contained only by the scope and limit of the creative imagination and the commitment it secures from those who believe in its power. All of the accomplishments of man find their genesis inside of the mind and flow out of the unlimited creative power of the imagination. Man is limited only by his ability to think and then by his skill to share his brainchild. Through communication and with emotional maturity, he might influence the collective efforts first by finding the courage to convince his family and second his community.

From the mind and ideas of people flow the very concept of the mind; i.e., beliefs in religions, politics, national identities, knowledge, and the concept of self. The mind possesses the ability to fulfill self and presents this skill as a prophecy. Ideas emerge from the brains as fetuses emerge from a pregnant womb, and the difference between the two lies only in our knowledge of conception. Because ideas require active engagement to be actualized, they are neutral. Our ideas succeed when enough people believe in them and work to make them real. Similarly, ideas fail when they are not supported, and they lack self-sustaining resources.

Who is a man or what is the mind of man? Is man a brain, or is the person a set of ideas? If a man is a brain, then how and why do many brains come to accept a single idea and conspire to make it real? Unquestionably, the ability to communicate effectively is second only to the power of the imagination. Think of an idea and convince enough people; then watch the idea take shape and life. History records the following ideas that had devastating results:

1.   1937 the Nanking Massacre.

Competitions were held between Japanese soldiers to see who could murder one hundred Chinese civilians the fastest with simply the use of a sword. About 300,000 human beings lives were lost in this ordeal.

2.   1945 the bombing of Hiroshima and Nagasaki.

The effect of the bombing resulted in 90,000 to 146,000 deaths in Hiroshima and 39,000 to 80,000 deaths in Nagasaki.

3.   1916 the Battle of Somme.

Inside twelve hours of a British offensive, 19,240 British soldiers lay dead within about 25 square miles after being slaughtered.

4.   1932 to 1933 the Holodomor.

Josef Stalin's famine a human right violation that most figures estimate led to the slaughter of between 4 - 5 million Ukrainian's, who starved to death during the Holodomor.

5.   1939 to 1945 the Holocaust.

Adolf Hitler's Nazi party routinely rounded up, enslaved, and exterminated six million Jews.

6.   1994 the Rwandan Genocide.

The rival Hutu majority slaughtered an estimated one million of the Tutsi tribe in Rwanda during 100 days.

7.   1958 to 1961 the Great Leap Forward.

Chairman Mao Zedong of China caused the death of millions of Chinese citizens.

8.   Late 17th and 18th Century.

Estimates are that about 12 to 12.8 million Africans were shipped across the Atlantic Ocean over 400 years into slavery.

9.   1492 Depopulation of the indigenous American population.

From 1491 to 1691, the population of indigenous Americans was systematically decimated by 90 to 95 percent, from approximately 145 million to 15 million people.

Ideas in human beings are like seeds in plants. People are idea factories and the seeds from our imaginations are filled with unlimited potentials. However, they produce when we have the knowledge, skill, and attitude to nurture them to fruition. The seed of an effective idea communicated effectively takes on a life of its own, and over time, matures into a significant marker in history. History records the following ideas that have disrupted the trajectory of human existence and societies:

1.   Writing

Writing is possibly the single most powerful invention birthed from the human mind. The invention of writing and eventually printing meant that ideas could be stored, explained, and transferred. Writing changed the way humans think. If we re-imagine the meaning of immortality, writing might be the first real step taken down this path.

2.   1890s Aviation.

German engineer, Otto Lilienthal glider flights, were the precursor to Orville and Wilbur Wright's pursuit and development of the aircraft in 1903. These inventions changed the way human traveled and made much of modern global crossing possible.

3. 1959 Lunar 2 Mission.

The first human-made object to reach the surface of the Moon was the Soviet Union's Luna 2 mission, on 13 September 1959 followed by the United States' Apollo 11 first crewed mission to land on the Moon, on 20 July 1969. Man learned that it is possible to exist beyond the surface of our planet.

4. 17th Century.

At the turn of the 17th century, English scientist William Gilbert established the science underlying the study of electricity and magnetism. Benjamin Franklin conducted his famous kite experiment to demonstrate that lightning was electricity in 1752. Joseph Henry and Edward Davy invented the remote switch and made modern telegraphy possible. Joseph Swan and Thomas Edison developed the practical light bulb in the late 1800s and changed the way humans live.

5. 1796 Smallpox vaccine.

Edward Jenner introduced the first successful vaccine with the use of material from cowpox pustules in 1796. Jenner was preceded by Chinese work with vaccines as early as 1000 CE and followed by Louis Pasteur's 1885 rabies vaccine. Understanding vaccines made it possible for people to thrive in modern cities.

Since ideas are ubiquitous, it is important for us to understand the critical factors that make some ideas succeed while others fail. An obvious characteristic of successful ideas is that they achieve mass appeal. Enough people must buy-in for an idea to succeed. Mass appeal is especially important when the cost of creation is a factor or when the idea runs counter to conventional wisdom. Where cost is a concern, the willingness to subsidize the production and promotion of the idea is an obvious concern in its development, promotion, and sustainability.

Whenever ideas run counter to conventional wisdom and cost is not an immediate concern achieving critical mass quickly is the primary concern. Therefore, as ideas trend toward achieving critical mass quickly, people go into an emotionally driven feeding frenzy. The frenzy produces irrational exuberance that might have catastrophic results. The mass killings in history are examples of ideas and people in frenzied situations.

Ideas sometimes gain traction because they have voices and faces that are effective. People who have transformative qualities can sell both good and bad ideas to others who are susceptible to influences. Susceptibility is predicated on the perception of needs. Whenever people feel vulnerable, at any level, transformative salespeople with messages that appeal to the vulnerability can sell them ideas.

Ideas mixed with fear are amplified in an echo chamber that drives people into an emotional frenzy. Only knowledge and reasoning stand in the way of irrational exuberance. Unfortunately, intellectuals who might be the gatekeepers of reason tend to have lower transformative appeal than eloquent and transformative leaders, and they are perceived as part of the bourgeoisie. Therefore, intellectuals tend to have less influence over the opinions of the masses.

There are no simple solutions to filtering ideas. By design, human beings are idea factories. We refer to the innate need for ideas as dreams, vision, purpose, goals, and objectives. People are considered to be lost whenever they are unable to define their dreams, vision, purpose, goals, or objectives. Therefore, ideas are as much a part of the human experience as leaves are to trees. The well-being of our species hinges on our ability to harness our resources and educate each other about the values and principles that promote our collective welfare.

We must embrace the rigors of science and the principles of arts, and use them to inform a common sense approach to selecting ideas about possibilities versus necessities. It is worth repeating the impact that collective learning has on the growth and evolution of groups.

Understanding the philosophy of the hundredth monkey might help us to grasp how Homo sapiens leaped to the top of the food chain. In theory mankind is a weak animal, yet today he is the master of the animal kingdom. Because enough sapiens learned valid knowledge the life of the species changed. The growth and life of human beings exemplify the relationship between knowledge and growth. Remember that in the beginning man lived in caves, in small groups, and fought to survive. He fought the elements; had no permanent home, and more than likely, he did not grow old.

After enough sapiens learned to domesticate animals and to cultivate crops; man stopped wandering and created homes. The new knowledge man learned about farming enabled the collective to transform the lifestyle of the group. The results of having new knowledge are communities, metropolis, countries, and federations.

Most importantly, when people stayed in place long enough, they created the time and space in which to learn and share their new learning. Man learned to write, and so he made it possible for knowledge to be stored and passed on to succeeding generations. The net result is we learn and grow at a much faster rate. Our species now face a new challenge. We must learn how to control the rate and direction of our growth. Simply taking a blind leap because it is possible might be too great of a gamble and might take our species over the edge and into an abyss.

The end.

ESSAY 5 INTELLIGENCE AND COMMUNICATION IN SAPIENS

In Homo sapiens' race and ethnic affiliation; color, class, and nationality are less important in defining differences between people than the similarity and shared characteristics in our brains. Intuitively one might argue that the most important resource and an asset to the singer is the voice, to the pianist are the fingers, to the runner are the legs, to the photographer are the eyes, and following such logic, the brain should be most important only to the people whose profession focuses on ideas. In fact, the brain is the most important asset to every person in all professions. Voices can be retrained only with a functioning brain and similarly the fingers, arms, legs, and eyes.

As man merges with machines, many of the previously indispensable limbs are being replaced with artificial creations. Today we have people who function with artificially created eyes, ears, arms, fingers, and legs. What all people need to fulfill their potential are functioning brains. The healthy brain is the person and the potential. The brain is a human being.

While race, gender, and national identities are used to define people and their places in the world, we share the same color at our core. All healthy brains have gray matter connected with white matter, nerve fibers, black substantia nigra, and red blood vessels. Therefore, the real me and you, like every healthy human brain on our planet, are gray, white, black, and red. We begin with these colors, and everything else might someday become a feature or function that we can exchange and customize.

When Homo sapiens evolve to being Homo Machina, the brain might be the only current organ in the body that makes it into the future. Immortality, as we understand it today, is the quest to preserve the identity, awareness, and function of the human brain. The physical characteristics of our brains are fairly similar. The average human brain weighs approximately 2.8 pounds with slight weight variance by gender and developed differences influenced by environments. Since Homo sapiens have more similarities than differences, why do personalities differ so much?

Our measure of people's intelligence represents the most observable difference in our understanding. Whenever we measure performance, attitudes, skills, and accomplishments; we are making judgments about some category of human intelligence. To date, our concept of human intelligence includes three basic categories; Abstract intelligence, which is the ability for verbal and symbolic thinking; Mechanical intelligence, which is the ability to effectively control your body and manipulate objects; and Social intelligence, which is the ability to communicate with people, understanding and performing in social relations.

This broad grouping of intelligence in human beings was postulated by the American psychologist Edward Lee Thorndike in 1920. In 1983 Howard Gardner described eight kinds of intelligence that in fact fit within these same groups. According to Gardner, intelligence can be described as; spatial, linguistic, kinesthetic, mathematical, interpersonal, musical, intrapersonal, and naturalistic.

There is an unfolding debate about the role of individual intelligence in social and professional success. Emotional intelligence or EQ, the measure of intrapersonal and interpersonal intelligence, is being promoted as the most important skill for people to develop. Our current concept of EQ was developed by Salovey and Mayer in the 1990s. However, the careful analysis of the measures of success in human beings can be reduced to a core idea and skill, i.e., the ability of the brain to communicate first with self and secondly socially and professionally.

Regardless of where one ranks in any particular intelligence or in the aggregate measure of intelligence, the ability to imagine concepts or use the creative imagination, encode and transmit the ideas; and listen and understand feedback is paramount for success.

All Homo sapiens experience twenty-four hours in each day regardless of the time zone in which he or she lives. How each person uses time most certainly differs, and their accomplishments serve as the evidence of their choices. Understanding and using the intelligence that promotes effective communications provides immeasurable advantages to people. The ability to communicate is a learnable skill and can be developed from experiences within the environment.

The quality of the nurturing and the environmental conditions one experiences during the formative years prepare us with the knowledge and skills, and by extension, fosters the attitude we use to navigate social and professional interactions. Learning to communicate at an early age is advantageous, but one can learn to communicate at any age. Without question, a person with a healthy brain is limited or empowered by his or her ability to communicate.

Communication is much more than sending ideas by messaging. Effective communication includes the ability to listen and understand; encode and decode ideas; and intuitively interact with other brains to build trust, dependency, and to foster respect. Whenever people limit their methods of communication to the use of machines, they inadvertently limit their development of natural communication skills. In Homos sapiens, practice improves knowledge and skill, and if we do not use our faculties, we lose our abilities.

The end.

ESSAY 6 MATURITY AND INTELLIGENCE IN HOMO SAPIENS

The physical growth and development stages in human beings are illustrative of more than biological markers. According to literature, there are at least nine distinct stages in the psychology of lifespan. The Lifespan stages are; prenatal, infancy, early childhood, middle childhood, adolescence, early adulthood, middle adulthood, late adulthood, and death and dying. For the sake of simplicity, we might group the stages as infancy, childhood, adolescence, and adulthood.

The stages are physically and biologically obvious yet we must understand that as human beings grow and mature physically, they move simultaneously through stages of motor abilities, social abilities, and cognitive development. All of the stages of growth and development have specific referent knowledge, skills, and behaviors. Therefore, raising healthy human beings requires the nurturing of both the physical and cognitive needs in people.

Although we find it helpful to analyze the stages in isolation and with distinct points of transitions, the stages unfold differently in people, with less clarity, and at different rates. Nutrition, lifestyle, and environment are important factors that affect human growth and development.

Maturity in human beings is the qualitative and quantitative measure of aggregate intelligence or specific intelligence. Therefore, people might be categorized as dependent, immature, functional, or mature in the respective areas of intelligence; mechanical, abstract, and social. These three groupings represent the broad categories of intelligence identified by Thorndike in 1920. According to David Weschler, intelligence is a person's capacity to be purposeful in action, rational in thoughts, and relate with the environment effectively.

Advances in our understanding of intelligence have allowed us to isolate specific intelligence, define the underlying knowledge and skills; and develop the habits that will produce the attitudes of maturity in each area. The goal of human actualization is to achieve maturity in knowledge, skill, and behavior. Being mature means we are independent in all areas of intelligence and able to work interdependently within the human collective.

The areas of multiple intelligence proffered by Howard Gardner and the most recent attention given to the study of emotional intelligence now seems to be common sense. Yet, we have taken years of study and significant evolution in ideas to arrive at this point of common sense. Every human child is born as a dependent, filled with potential for intelligence, and immature. Babies are mechanically, spatially, and socially immature. Babies begin their intelligence journey as dependents and who they become is the direct function of the quality and quantity of exposure and interaction they experience in their environments. The quality of exposure children have to the aggregate and individual intelligence determines to a great extent who the mature version of the child might become.

Homo sapiens are not definitively determined by the factors in their environment, but they are influenced to a large extent by the things they experience in their formative years. Our self-awareness and intrapersonal skills, underlying components of social and emotional intelligence, enables us to influence the impact that externalities might have on our growth and development.

The end.

ESSAY 7 PECULIARITY IN OUR SPECIES

The most admirable human qualities flow out of our intelligences. The behaviors in others that we admire are the reflections of our innate capabilities, and especially the skills that we believe are underdeveloped in self. The apparent intelligence and example of exemplar in each category follows:

1. Spatial intelligence as the visual arts in pictures. Leonardo da Vinci,

2. Linguistic intelligence as a verbal skill. Martin Luther King, Jr.,

3. Kinesthetic intelligence in dancing and sport. Michael Jordan,

4. Mathematical intelligence as logical reasoning, the solving of puzzles. Einstein,

5. Interpersonal intelligence as relationship skills. Oprah Winfrey,

6. Musical intelligence in the production of music. Beethoven,

7. Intrapersonal intelligence self-awareness and introspection. Gautama Buddha, and

8. Naturalistic intelligence in exploring the outdoors. Ibn

Battuta.

People recognize the innate characteristics of our species and seek out others who might serve as exemplars. One challenge to this practice of identifying and admiring exemplars is the tendency to set their level of performance beyond the reach of our capabilities. We tend to use exemplars as justification for our lack of discipline and dedication to realizing our potential in our intelligence.

People say they desire specific outcome in different areas of life yet, by action, they contradict their own yearnings. Naturally, we want the best for self and our interests. The desire for a healthy and happy life is the most basic human need, yet, approximately one billion people are daily smokers. The smoking habit might be the most obvious contradictory human behavior. Smoking is an unquestionable slow and deliberate path to illness and eventually, death. Smoking is simultaneously pleasurable. Smokers rationalize that everyone dies eventually and that they deserve the pleasure or relief they get from the habit. Therefore, the choice to smoke might be no more a poor decision than the decision to travel on the interstates of any country where people meet tragic accidents every day.

On this single contradiction, smoking, roughly twenty percent of the world's population makes questionable choices. As a fact, we live out of our heads. Human beings live in their heads and all experiences pre and post stimuli are processed in the brain. The brain is the single source of awareness in human existence. Our contradictions are evidence of the peculiarity in the decision-making process of human beings. If we have challenge committing to the support of such a fundamental need, surviving by stop smoking, then our decision-making process regarding less significant needs will be difficult. Smoking is a life issue and a much more important decision than social or professional choices. Are there explanations for this flaw in our system?

The peculiarity in human nature that allows the majority of people to settle for less than their full potential needs to be explored and understood. If a man is guided by factors that might harm him, the desire to smoke, then how do we evaluate and navigate the choices that are in our best interest? Man designs machines and gadgets to meet specific purposes. Cars are designed as transportation; houses to live in, speakers to produce sound, boats to sail, planes to fly, and pets are raised for the amusement of the owners. If our cars crushed us deliberately or our pets ate us, we would eliminate them from our lives. Whenever our computers fail to compute, we replace the broken machine. Whenever any of our creations fail to satisfy the purpose for which they are intended, we consider them as broken and in need of repair or replacement. Yet, at the human level, when people fail to live up to their designed purpose, we rationalize. I imagine that to rationalize is, in reality, to convince self and others with rational lies.

The peculiarity and contradiction in human nature would be considered as a glitch in our machines. People make war to create peace. Human beings live multiple ideas simultaneously because we are complex beings. We are able to subordinate facts and logic to satisfy the concepts and ideas. We need to understand which of our ideas deserve preeminence, develop a system of prioritization, and personal discipline.

This is our search to understand the meaning of our existence.

We toil in the physical realm to support the lives in our heads, and whenever our actions lead us on diverging paths, we rationalize, become depressed, or adjust. Only a small number of people take steps and realigns their physical activities to meet the objectives in their heads. Every man and woman on the planet who has a healthy brain has a dream or personal goal. Based on the conditions of his or her circumstances, the dream might range from the need to have safety and security to be at the pinnacle of actualization. However, the majority of people subordinates their personal desires and elevates the goals of other people or corporations above their own. They invariably volunteer for subjugation. A dream is of value only when we invest in its realization.

In reality, humans do the things that they believe. We operate based on values and without clear conviction in our beliefs, we often subvert the development of beneficial habits. Our multiple intelligences are not physical or obvious to the untrained mind. Intelligence is deep cognitive knowledge and skills that become evident only when we develop the requisite habits. The habits are displayed as attitudes, and intelligence appears as a character trait. Developing intrapersonal intelligence is a possible important step toward improving the overall well-being and decision-making in our species.

The end.

ESSAY 8 THE RELEVANCE OF KNOWLEDGE TO HOMO SAPIENS

The knowledge of Homo sapiens is only as important as it is relevant to our wellbeing. This means that as a best practice, we should assess the value of our knowledge as it correlates to our skills. Our skills must relate to behaviors and habits that produce satisfaction in our important endeavors. We might use Abraham Maslow's hierarchy of needs to describe our common levels of needs; physiological needs, safety needs, love and belonging, self-esteem needs, and self-actualization. Skills that help us to satisfy the needs in our lives are important in our wellbeing and skills are supported by knowledge. People are proficient at the things they understand. Without knowledge, good performance is an accident.

The brain is the seat of consciousness and the single source of awareness in human beings. All other organs in the human body send signals to the brain and respond to instructions from the brain. Although many bodily functions seem to occur automatically, in reality, they operate from subconscious brain directives. Essentially, some activities execute below the threshold of primary awareness. The brain is in total control of the person, and its influence cannot be overstated. Man is trapped within the confines of his knowledge and might have been called a *"Looper"* because his condition is that of existential looping. Man develops and matures by learning new and relevant knowledge, through learning we grow.

Consider the existence of any person as a circle. The perimeter represents the existing limit of a person's knowledge. Keep in mind that knowledge translates to skills. Therefore, a person who does not use his or her skill might overtime lose the associated dexterity. Another person might, through learning decide to specialize and deliberately reduce the size of his or her circle. Some knowledge has the influence of constricting the overall intelligence of people. In other words, one might become dumber because of what one learns, believes, and practice. Many ideas, such as racist philosophy fall into the "make you dumber" category.

Conversely, ideas that expand your circle are growth ideas. Being trapped inside of your idea and inside the head is a relative term. Because knowledge is the limit of the person what we know is all that we are. The aggregate knowledge is inevitably much more than individual knowledge. Hence, we are so much more when we share resources and work interdependently. Constricting ideas are breaking in ideas that force people inward and downward. These are limiting thoughts and systems of beliefs that contradict the natural working of principles. Expanding ideas are breaking out ideas. These are concepts of values that inherently support the natural laws and principles of the universe. They force us upward and outward. The knowledge of the man or woman who is growing gets larger, and he or she develops new skills and become more effective at doing old things.

Understanding the skill set of a person provides an important window into understanding the limits of his or her knowledge. For example, a person who had a dysfunctional family life or who had limited social relationships might lack the skills that are necessary for effective teamwork. He or she may not have learned the knowledge that reinforces the merits of teamwork. Any man who stands apart and alone might feel secure in his mind. His idea of security is an illusion constructed on limiting mindset and knowledge. The willingness to trust others and to grow is the result of being open to learning new knowledge. Therefore, the obsessive pursuit of achieving emotional and financial independence and avoidance of emotional commitment is evidence of background and experience of lack and disappointment.

Our lives reflect the experiences we work to avoid consciously. The pursuit of independence is simply the other side of the avoiding dependence coin. Pursuing interdependence is the mature acceptance of social and emotional needs and working to fulfill the values of the abundance mentality.

Man as a species advance when we capitalize on shared ideas. In many cases, people form relationships around the idea, and they have no need to bond at a personal level. Corporations are economic pooling of ideas. The publicly traded corporation represents the interdependent financial power of teamwork. Cities, states, and countries represent the pooling of ideas. Within countries, people will divide themselves into groups by states, cities, neighborhoods, and social clubs; and they might elevate their common ideas above ideas outside their immediate circle.

Similarly, the aggregation of ideas might give rise to concerns. Ideas are sometimes more powerful than individuals and seem to take on lifelike qualities. Whatever we value informs our system of thinking. How we think becomes our paradigm, the way we see things. Therefore, the limit of our knowledge informs our ability to learn, understand, and to grow.

The end.

ESSAY 9 GROWTH AND GENERALIZED INTELLIGENCE IN HOMO SAPIENS

What does it mean when people grow? Whenever we say someone has grown, we mean he or she might have increased in size; literal growth, or in stature by earning respect. Growth might be measured in spiritual or emotional terms. Physical growth is influenced by biology and can be moderated by lifestyle; exercise and diet, to some extent. However, there are obvious limits to how much physical growth is possible in a person. Physical growth is a quantitative measure, while emotional and spiritual growths are decisions people make in the imaginative realm. Both are qualitative measures of change.

The creative imagination and the courage to explore self are the only two obvious limits to how much emotional and spiritual growth are possible in people. When people grow in stature, their external image changes, and the measure of their growth is directed from the external towards the person. One can choose to learn and develop spiritual and emotional practices that will affect one's stature. Stature depends on the opinions of other people. Our emotional deportment and spiritual practices define our image.

Spirituality is a fluid and subjective concept. Emotions are constructs of conditioning and often appear to be automatic responses that flow out of people as a result of stimuli. Emotional and spiritual growths push cognition into the sphere of limitlessness and include many layers of experiences. In Homo sapiens, social and emotional intelligence represents an immeasurable window into the potential for growth and who we might become.

Growth means we push past the limits of our known intelligence and into unknown spaces. We have limited understanding of the intricate details in all of our intelligences and how we measure them. However, intelligence represents the different areas in our lives where we have the potential for growth and development. It is linked to our senses and includes every area of decision-making where we can identify life stage development.

The antithesis to growth is decline and eventual death. Growth happens when people assimilate new knowledge and translate the knowledge to practices and habits. Therefore, in Homo sapiens, the observable areas of growth are physical, spiritual, and emotional. Physical growth includes automatic biological development and possibly growth from personal conditioning. Spiritual and emotional growth occurs from the condition, and conditioning is influenced by experience. Growing can occur in a mutually exclusive area, all areas, or in a combination of any areas. The distribution of growth over the whole person can vary; therefore; the experience of growth might be uniquely personalized. Growing is the opposite of decline, and the end state of progressive decline is death. The end state of progressive growth is limitless and difficult to quantify.

In the spiritual sense, growth is an extension of survival. Survival is the first step on the stairway of life and growth functions as a marker that one crosses at each step moving upward. Surviving is a basic human desire in all healthy brains. The most effective tool that supports growth is emotional dissatisfaction with the present conditions and the recognition of a gap between the current state and a desirable ideal.

Ignorance about limits helps one to tap into the subconscious resources of the brain and to engage the power of the creative imagination. This means that it is possible to be limited by the knowledge you possess. The creative imagination in man is his most powerful resources when it is used effectively. Imagination must be fed a healthy diet of possibilities. The mind must be educated and nurtured with healthy values and principle-based information. Whenever people consume a diet with useless data and information constantly, the result is a decline in intelligence.

People define their goals in their creative imagination, and the subconscious function of the brain identifies, interprets, and produces conditions that satisfy the criteria for success. From the emotion, people must reinforce the conditions for growth with the courage to engage with new experiences. Growth in human beings means change and dictates the abandonment of static philosophies of life. Growth is internal, yet moves the mind and body through experiences in the external environment. One might grow and remain within the same physical space because the change unfolds out of personal paradigm.

Whenever we adopt the growth mindset, and we are living in the mode of growth, we are creating our experiences. We acquire data, disassemble what we learn, and reassemble the knowledge into whatever we need to change our state of mind. At first, growth might occur as a slow revelation of the possibilities. Our rate of growth should increase after we develop the habit of seeking growth, and we are intentional about working to achieve specific growth objectives. In the interdependent reality, where people choose to create in teams, the power of growth is amplified and sapiens produce innovative ideas and disruptive technologies.

In Homo sapiens thinking requires references. The human brain is a biological compass, and for learning to happen points of reference provide context for the processing of data and information. References are produced through experience and studying. References allow people to navigate and position themselves about whatever they are taking in. Without references, people would be disoriented and lost with new and meaningless data. All of our concepts and ideas are developed about our senses and the underlying intelligence. In human beings, the common concept of our senses refers to the external sensors that support the qualitative and quantitative interpretation of stimuli from the environment.

Man can conceive, perceive, and understand only concepts for which he has points of references. The relevance; validity and reliability, of the references, determine the quality and accuracy of the markers for intelligence growth that are laid down in the brain. References are the knowledge; data, and information, which lead back to the inherent intelligence that supports whatever is being learned. References can be learned through experience and study. However, learning occurs because one has the underlying intelligence that supports the new knowledge.

Consequently, the absence of the requisite intelligence in people hinders the development and learning of new knowledge. Education is the nurturing and development of inherent reasoning abilities in people. It might be possible for people to develop new cognitive abilities. However, the assumption is that people must have the inherent characteristic that supports the growth and development of any new intelligence. Without the required capacity to perform a function, there is nothing to develop. Intelligent machines have skills that are programmed based on the logic of design.

The use of pure logic or machine reasoning is the attempt to engage intelligence without the underlying and requisite characteristics and markers. True intelligence is measurable and has both qualitative and quantitative properties. Any assumptions about intelligence that are based on logic and quantitative derivatives without qualitative properties represent artificial intelligence, AI. People can develop skills and learn to think like machines; however, until we create machines with intuition and emotions, they cannot function like people. We can behave like machines because we possess the characteristics and markers for machine intelligence. AI is a human creation.

Machine intelligence is based on logic and reasoning, and it is a regressive capability when compared to the creative imagination of human beings. The specialized functions in AI support efficiencies but lack the generalized capabilities of human intelligence. Growth in human is predicated on the presence of biological markers that contain at least traces for the genus of the intelligence. A tree does not grow from a lifeless rock because the properties of life are organic.

In Homo sapiens, intelligence is wired into our biology, and it develops through learning. In machines, intelligence has to be programmed and is dependent on logic. Whenever we use machine thinking and decision-making, we might be achieving a new stage in efficiency, but we are essentially diminishing the inherent capabilities of our generalized intelligence.

The end.

ESSAY 10 PRESERVING HOMO SAPIENS: SPECIES EXEMPLARS FROM EXTINCTION

The rate of machinization of Homo sapiens has increased, and today's species of man might cease to exist much sooner than we imagine. With no natural competitors, the species exemplar, Homo sapiens, with the use of his imagination are creating their replacement. If our model of the future includes a rational, thinking, and introspective human being, then an intervention is needed to protect our species. Thoughts emerge from the brain. Sow a thought produce an action. Disciplined actions produce habits, and with enough effective habits in the whole person, the character of the human evolves.

The personality of the human being is the aggregate of factors that influence character. Our species share numerous overlapping character traits. How we use technologies and the habits we are creating are changing the character of our species. We recognize and discuss the digital divides, and this means our species is now evolving differently based on social class and economic status. Ignorance, insensitivity, low intuition, and data-driven habits lower our inherent intelligence. People who become dependent on technologies develop difficulties thinking and interacting socially. As our species outsource more of our introspective skills to our machines, we diminish and eventually lose the ability to communicate effectively.

We have all experienced indifference in social interaction when people in social settings stare at us with blank and lifeless expression. We might have even acted indifferent to others, and if you would prefer to work from home instead of with a team in the office, you might have already begun adapting the machine's attitude. Machines lack social and emotional intelligence. The obsession with data-driven decision-making is further evidence of this problem in our society.

The desire to improve is not a strategy for improving. Having an accurate mental model of the intended outcome is one of the most important factors in a workable strategy. Second is having the emotional intelligence to select and focus on the priorities that support the achievement of the intended goal. There is a healthy point of balance between controlling our machines and being controlled by data, information, and machines.

Data-driven relationships are invariably impersonal, while humanized metrics are based on introspection. People have intelligence that allows them to be introspective. Machines are unable to humanize decision-making. In our quest to produce comfort, we imagine a future with humanized machines, and because of our limitations, we machinize human as a compromise. We must intervene in how we and successive generations balance the human-machine relationship before we become machine-dependent completely.

In the abyss of the machinized future, only machines will possess the ability to analyze our maladies because our appraisals will be too complex and data-centric for us to understand. At such time our species will be subordinate to pure reasoning and logic. In the future of the mechanized world where men become the eyes, ears, and legs; the sensors, the machines will be the brains and our species will be disposable and irrelevant.

In the abyss; the age of true machines with AI as primary decision-makers, a man might cease to be relevant. Beyond biology, the only significant difference between people is the factors of intelligence; mechanical, social, and spatial. People have experience and conditioning that make them seem different, but we have the same potentials. We have multiple intelligences and are at different levels of maturity and skill levels.

Our knowledge and experiences determine what we know and value. It is easy to live in a loop; in our heads, and accomplish nothing simply because we do not know what we do not know. We have to study constantly and make decisions with the long view in mind. I have concluded that our creative imagination and self-awareness are important when we are choosing to change but having accurate mental models of the future are critical for us to survive.

The end.

ESSAY 11 SOCIAL AND EMOTIONAL INTELLIGENCE IN HOMO SAPIENS

In Homo sapiens, intelligence includes the building blocks for knowledge, habits, and character. With valid knowledge, people create habits. Habits aggregate to produce character and personalities, and by extension, the attitudes of people. In psychology, intelligence represents one's ability and motivation to learn. People can develop social and emotional knowledge and habits and improve their socio-emotional intelligence. While some people seem to have a natural gift for establishing relationships, others might have to work to develop and maintain the skill. All people use social habits and have a basic need to interact with others. Social habits and characteristics are inherent and necessary for the development of healthy personalities.

In our societies, newborns first learn to interact with an inner circle such as family members and then they develop associations with an expanding circle of people. Babies internalize the emotion for trust through social interaction.

People who fail to develop healthy relationships over time experience social isolation and emotional challenges. People who have low social skills possess less developed social and emotional habits and by extension, lower social and emotional intelligence. Earning above-average scores on social and emotional intelligence assessment does not automatically mean one will be comfortable in all interpersonal interactions. Instead, it means that one has the general skills to navigate interpersonal relationships. This is the same as being functionally literate in the social and emotional categories.

Introversion and extroversion are major measures of personality traits and represent social intelligence. Introversion represents low sociability, and extroversion represents high sociability skills. Regardless of where one ranks on the social scale, social intelligence is a feature of the human experience. Whether social intelligence is low or high in people merely represents the level of development one has in social knowledge, skills, and habit. Social relations are measured based on the emotional impact they have on people; therefore, social intelligence and emotional intelligence share overlapping constructs. According to research, social intelligence represents common sense and tact. The experiences of human beings are expressed as emotions.

Generally, we discuss emotions as if they are natural and instinctive states of mind. In fact, emotions are constructed by people in responses to stimuli, and they flow out of conditioning. Emotions appear to be instinctive because they are cognitive codes that execute in the subconscious mind below the threshold of primary awareness. Social skills are necessary for the navigating of interpersonal relationship roles. Emotional intelligence represents the ability to understand and manage personal feelings and the emotional impact of interactions in social relationships. The importance of social and emotional intelligence in human interaction is common sense because socializing is a significant and common part of human experience.

Although people share similar social experience, each person's opinion and experience is uniquely personal. No two people experience the same qualitative measure of emotional experience because emotions are constructed within each brain. However, people use internal constructs of values, to define and agree on the merits of their social and emotional experience. Experiencing pain is an emotional concept with no unifying or quantitative objective measure. The only measure of pain that is shared by all human beings is its presence or absence. In the core of human existence, the presence and absence of each emotion define our opinion of our experiences. The experiences of life are unique to each person, and out of this individuality, people construct emotions.

Similarly, values and norms represent concepts of judgment about shared ideas and ideological references. Much of how human interpret experiences with qualitative qualifiers such as good, bad, happy, and sad are subjective emotional constructions. Values are the qualitative representations of the meaning of experiences. Concepts such as money, patriotism, national identity, race, religion, social unit, and political beliefs; are examples of values people might share and use to define social and emotional structures. Values are important in the human experience because they enable ideas to get from inside of a brain and across the collective. Values influence habits because they are the basis of decision-making and prioritizing in human beings. Human behavior flows out of their perception of values. Values provide a common reference in human experience. People use values to justify the compromises they make to get beyond inherent selfish ideas and through the automatic survival mechanisms that are hardwired into our species.

Values can be weaponized with eloquence. People with transformative communication skills understand how to package and present values that appeal to people. Pride is a unifying value like religious doctrines, political ideologies, and patriotism. Communication is effective when they reflect values packaged as stories. Stories tend to be accessible, and when we learn them, we share them easily and freely. Hence, values can be contagious. Values provide meaning to our stories and lives. Sometimes values might inversely influence behavior; therefore, effective communication is a science.

Effective communicators link values to the behavior they seek from people and use them as triggers to instigate action. Successful ideas are about deliberate and personal conditioning. In conditioning, we use habitual practices to move ideas from mind-state to subconscious and automatic behaviors that flow below our threshold of primary decision-making. Negative reinforcement is one form of conditioning. Social and emotional intelligence is developed through ideological conditioning. Values develop from beliefs. Beliefs evolve from practices and emotional assumptions. Assumptions are reinforced by expectations. Expectations evolve from our knowledge, and there are no definitive ways to separate our ideas from our experiences. Values can be internalized through practice, and the net result is conditioning.

Leaders of organizations and groups who define core values, and use them to indoctrinate the followers, condition the followers to respond to value-based triggers. The triggers can be used to elicit specific behaviors. All of our habits flow out of conditioning. People carry multiple values simultaneously.

In Homo sapiens, the operative idea of value is a system. Values affect the behaviors of people. Therefore, when people learn to prioritize, they develop an intelligence supporting skill. Many people are unaware of all of their values. People have habits that they do not understand and cannot explain. Herein lays the challenge people face in the pursuit of their stated goals. Most people work tirelessly in pursuit of things that do not support their stated purpose or goal. Just as many people make decisions that contradict their stated objectives, and they are convinced that the elements in nature are conspiring to prevent them from achieving their goals. In reality, when people have values that they do not recognize their subconscious system still work to make them real.

The subconscious mind does everything to satisfy the values even when they seem to contradict overt thoughts. The brain is the single most powerful organ in the human body. The brain will sacrifice every other organ and even the whole person in pursuit of its cranial satisfaction. All stories of successes and failures begin and end in the brain. Homo sapiens imagine, believe, and act; they confirm and contradict values against principles.

Whenever ideas are consistent with principles, success is assured. Habits are both good and bad in as much as they promote the wellbeing or demise of the person. Twenty percent of the world's populations are daily smokers. Approximately eight million people die from smoking-related illnesses annually. Smoking is a habit, and the choice to smoke is value-based. Smoking is a social habit that provides emotional rewards. The most effective approach to managing socio-emotional needs is the establishment of a compelling mental map. Mental maps that are value-based provide the brain with subconscious reasons to produce fulfilling behaviors and habits.

The end.

ESSAY 12 OUR VALUES AND EMOTIONS

All behaviors in human, ranging from bad, indifferent, to good are values on an emotional scale of our creation. Emotions represent one's assessment of feeling in response to stimuli. One genius in our species is this ability to build up abstract ideas and make them into important cornerstones in our societies. We refer to many such emotional values as constitutions and religious doctrines. Many of man's ideas and emotional values achieve such prominence that people are jailed and even executed for violating these sacred ideas.

Emotion presents a conundrum for people who lack the knowledge to understand its meaning because they believe feelings of sadness, joy, and optimism simply flow out of the brains of men. People who study and understand the psychology of emotions recognize the classic chicken or egg first predicament with the emotions question. If people construct their emotions based on their knowledge and experiences, then, we should have people who expect and accept ill-treatment as normal behavior from abusive partners. An iteration of this is referred to as victim mentality.

Victim mentality is the learn state where people become conditioned to expect victimization, and they function in the constant state of expecting to be abused, sometimes contrary to the evidence. Another example of the emotional condition might be chronic pain syndrome, especially in people who develop certain conditioned behavior long after the pain is lessened or resolved.

While these extreme instances or obsessive behaviors and compulsions fit neatly into the area of emotional illness, they are symptomatic of the fact that all emotions develop out of one's expectation. In other words, emotions are, in fact, examples of the self-fulfilling prophecy in human being.

The scales people use to measure emotions are as valid as the basis of the origin of the experience. Because we have designed and developed scales of measure for assessments, we imagine that they are an accurate representation of concepts. In the confines of limited knowledge, we have no notion of factors that might contradict our measures. Since our scales are based on arbitrary values, the results are themselves arbitrary. Unless the scales of measure are established on natural principles, they are illusionary. Our current definition of emotions is a qualitative assumption about the values we share.

Our values evolve from experiences and conditioning. All of our scales are figments of our imagination and meaningless to people who do not share the values. No two people can pinpoint the numerical value of a specific emotion even when they experience the same event at the exact instant. The values we share are like currencies that we agree to accept. Therefore, values add meaning to human experiences. If as a society, we agree that adding the number one to three equals thirteen, then all successive generations will have this incorrect assumption about one and three.

Leaders in organizations frequently tout the need to have mission, vision, and core values. These are important in organizations because the mission, vision, and core values serve as the reference that the members of the organization should use to make a decision. Values in societies are exemplified by the rule of law and the expected codes of conduct.

Many societies have codes of standards that contradict each other because they evolve out of the conditioning and self-interest of the people who have the authority to make rules. In some religious text, slaves are urged to obey their masters. We can make a safe wager that people who benefited from owning slaves supported the inclusion of the statement in the religious texts.

Similarly, men who felt the need to suppress women's rights promoted the argument that women must be subservient to men. On the surface, these appear to be divisive notions. However, they tell important stories when we assess them within the context of knowledge. We only understand emotional experiences. When people work to be logical and rational, their behavior is represented on an emotional scale because human beings are emotional animals.

Where do values come from? Are people born with values? Do we inherently have shared value systems? And do our values change? Every day people across the world work together, and in theory, they are pursuing common goals. Actually, only a minority of groups share the values that link people together in pursuit of common objectives. People are in the same building and heading in the same general direction in the physical space, but in their heads, there is less agreement. Sharing physical space does not mean people hope or expect to get the same results at the same point.

The greatest challenge in every group effort is finding common ground through the sharing of values. Individual survival is instinctive in the healthy brain and has to be suppressed when people hope to achieve a group objective. Where do group objectives come from?

People who have errant and incorrect ideas about emotion are like vinyl records with scratch marks. They are trapped in unhealthy and sometimes irrationally stupid loops. Ideas are not like wound that heal over time if they are cleaned and treated with care. Emotions are more like subtle infections that will keep coming back every time the triggers are experienced, and as long as the incorrect ideological assumptions remain in one's head. Emotional ideas cannot be surgically removed. Instead, they have to be replaced with more compelling ideas, and one must have mental maps that appeal to the subtleties of the subconscious mind.

In the human brain values function like programs in our machines. Replacing our values requires reformatting or overwriting of our hard drives.

The end.

ESSAY 13 CHOOSING TO WIN

I watched ants move the body of a large bug across a sidewalk. The ants covered approximately two inches of sidewalk in less than sixty seconds then spent over four minutes navigating the body of the bug over the edge of the sidewalk. The edge of the sidewalk must have appeared as a cliff in comparison to the size of the ants. At the edge of the cliff, the ants congregated around another ant as if to strategize and then they moved back and forth between the body of the bug and the group of ants. Eventually, they succeeded in taking the bug over the edge of the sidewalk and into the grass.

When everyone pulls in the same direction, and when people share values and knowledge, enormous and complex challenges are solved. Conversely, no parent, teacher, coach, or doctor can work hard enough to save and secure success for people who do not want to be saved or secured. The motivation to succeed must come from the brain of each person.

Homo sapiens have a biologically wired desire for self-preservation. Every interaction with external forces is assessed to determine the threat-level it might present. Therefore, people have difficulty being vulnerable and trusting others. We must learn to trust each other before we can give our best to each other. The lack of trust gets in the way of communication and the ability for teams to form and produce. Trust is important in interpersonal relationships and cohesive team performance. Without trust, people will never achieve the full potential of what is possible because we are stronger, more innovative, and safer in teams that include competent people.

With study and practice, healthy brains can grow and develop the capacity for improved performance. Study and practice are important because it is impossible to function beyond the capability of one's capacity. Homo sapiens have a creative imagination and inherent blind spots. The blind spots produce biases, but we can overcome these with our imagination.

The person who has never seen or heard of a Magdil can imagine one with an introduction from an external source. If I said, a Magdil is like an Avocado, you can imagine the shape, color, smell, taste, texture, and uses because you have a mental reference. Therefore, current limits serve merely as cautionary markers that identify the need for development. Your current knowledge, values, expectations, and experiences are not the limits of your potential. Instead, they are bridges that you can cross when you decide to increase your intelligence.

The ultimate goal is to work beyond your individual capacity like the ants. This means that after you achieve independent habits, you make a choice to embrace a mindset of interdependence. You choose to work in teams where you engage the introspective skills of human beings, and you seek to understand the needs of others before you impose your opinions.

Most important is that you relate with others from a principle-centered perspective and build relationships that are based on values. The values you choose must support the health and wellbeing of our species. When you commit to saving our species you will be saving yourself.

The end.

ESSAY 14 HOMO SAPIENS AS PRODUCERS AND CONSUMERS

Three key areas of focus for understanding human behaviors are the brain, imagination, and communication, BIC. The brain is the person and represents the entire concept of the individual. All other functions in the body support the operation of the brain both directly or indirectly. The brain is such an important part of the person that to date, we have not had a brain transplant. Preserve the human brain with its functionality and mankind achieves immortality.

In Homo sapiens, the key focus area in the body is the brain. The important behaviors that emerge from the brains are the abilities to imagine and create innovative ideas; interpret stimuli based on values and principles; and communicate expectation through actions and stories.

The knowledge one possesses is important in defining the experiences of life. The senses, sight, smell, taste, touch, and hearing; are secondary level factors in what and how one experience life. The primary and single most important factor in defining the quality of life is brain health. Through the brain, the senses gain definition. The ability to see, hear, smell, feel, and taste are not brain health; instead, they are brain wealth. These abilities expand the ability of the brain to experience, absorb, and learn new knowledge. With knowledge, the brain has a reservoir from which one can synthesize ideas. Based on the depth and breadth of one's knowledge emerge the capacity to interpret ideas or for innovations. The primary and secondary factors, combined with the knowledge of people, produce human intelligence. Our current understanding of intelligence fit them into three categories mechanical, abstract, and spatial.

From these three categories of intelligence, people develop the abilities for independent behavior and for communication. The ability to communicate is an important quality of life skill. Trust and respect are mediating factors in communication. The development of knowledge helps people to grow and work interdependently because they learn about the importance of community and collective participation. Growth and development can foster resentment when people learn about how they have been disadvantaged due to their lack of knowledge. The role of knowledge is important in intelligence, and the quality of the lifestyle people experience. Based on knowledge, people make a choice to be either producers or consumers.

In the societies of Homo sapiens, people fall into two distinct categories. These categories are producers and consumers. Producers create things, and they produce more than they consume. In the producers' lifestyle, there is always net gain of resources. Consumers can produce, but they consume more than they create. Sometimes consumers are engaged in producing as employees, and they experience a net loss of resources. In the producer and consumer relationship, there is a constant transfer of resources from consumers to producers. Consumers earn, but because of habit, they are constantly transferring their earning to producers. The result of this relationship is forty-four percent of global wealth is controlled by less than one percent of the world's population.

According to statistics, ten percent of adults control eighty-five percent of the world's wealth. Researchers have concluded that the social and economic mobility of children is similar to the experience of their parent. Therefore, children born to families in the lower ninety percent of the economic bracket have much greater climbing to complete before they can access the net producer class of citizenry. Knowledge and habits are important factors in social and economic mobility.

For consumers to access the social class of the producer class, they must become voracious consumers of knowledge and habitual net producers. Additionally, people in the consumer class must develop the emotional intelligence to avoid becoming angry and dispirited when they learn that although they might have shared physical spaces with producers, and might have worked on the same teams, their lack of knowledge might have resulted in them experiencing significant disadvantages. Producers must avoid the tendency to assume that environmental disadvantages for people in the consumer class mean lower intelligence and inherent ignorance. Such a mindset can produce resentment and social conflict.

Producers and consumers are brains with different advantages. Because our species share a collective fate; working together is in the best interest of those who consume and those who produce. Failure to accept this fact might plunge our species into a self –destructive chaos.

According to Marcus Garvey, "Intelligence rules the world while ignorance carries the burden." Michael Manley aptly stated that the greatest threat to the survival of our species is the widening gap between social classes. Therefore, we must learn how to learn and develop the mindset for producing in the interest of our species and the health of our planet.

The end.

ESSAY 15 A BRIEF HISTORY OF EMOTIONAL INTELLIGENCE

Intelligence is a measure of how people process stimuli and then make decisions within different areas of life. People make different types of decisions in daily life, and according to the American Psychological Association, (APA)," Intelligence refers to intellectual functioning." Within the intellect, there are categories of functions. Therefore, we have different categories of intelligence. The nature of our decisions might be abstract, mechanical, or social. Hence, psychologists have coined the phrases mechanical intelligence, abstract intelligence, and social intelligence. In 1920 American psychologist Edward Lee Thorndike proposed that intelligence involves three distinct abilities:

1. Abstract intelligence - the ability to verbal and symbolic thinking
2. Mechanical intelligence - the ability to effectively control your body and manipulate objects
3. Social intelligence - the ability to communicate with people, understand and perform in social relations.

Of course, the most commonly discussed intelligence is our intelligence quotient, (IQ), which is academic or cognitive intelligence. IQ is often used to describe the level of smartness. However, mechanical, abstract, and social intelligence represented the much larger basket of ideas, and their division produced the intelligence model described by Howard Gardner. In 1983 Gardner described eight kinds of intelligence:

1	Spatial intelligence (Visual)	painting pictures
2	Linguistic intelligence (Verbal)	writing stories, memorization, and speaking
3	Kinesthetic intelligence (Bodily)	dancing and sport –good hand and eye coordination
4	Mathematical intelligence (Logical)	recognizing patterns and solving mathematical problems
5	Interpersonal intelligence (People)	excellent relationship building –verbal and nonverbal communication
6	Musical intelligence (Music)	thinking in patterns rhythms, and sounds
7	Intrapersonal intelligence (Self)	self-awareness and introspection
8	Naturalistic intelligence (Nature)	camping, gardening, exploring the outdoors

In 1990 Salovey and Meyer developed the theory of emotional intelligence as a cognitive ability with four measurable abilities, including:

1. Perception of emotion,

2. Emotional facilitation,

3. Understanding emotions, and

4. Management of emotions

The link between the three concepts Thorndike, Gardner, and Salovey and

Mayer is obvious even to a casual observer. Gardner's eight kinds of intelligence broaden Thorndike's proposed model of intelligence.

Similarly, Salovey and Mayer's model builds on Gardner's intrapersonal and interpersonal intelligence and leads back to Thorndike's concept of social intelligence. With the development of the Mayer Salovey Emotional Intelligence Test, (MSCEIT), Thorndike's social intelligence moved from the realm of abstract science to being a measurable model. Bar-On's 2006 Emotional Quotient Inventory (EQ-i) reinforced the validity of emotional intelligence as a measurable model. However, the divergence between the measures in the MSCEIT and the EQ-i raised questions about whether emotional intelligence is a behavioral model or a traits model.

Arguably the question raises a moot point because decision-making in Homo sapiens is not within the exclusive realm of either reason and willpower, or emotions. Emotional intelligence, at its most basic, is about self-control in decision-making, and primarily in the interest of the future self. Some decisions require traits or behavioral approach or some combination of traits and behavioral approach; to achieve success. A more important argument in emotional intelligence is whether emotions are constructed from experience versus feelings that flow out of mind as a response to stimuli.

Regardless of where the emotional intelligence argument leads, Homo sapiens need a framework of foundational knowledge which they use in decision-making. The framework is the aggregate of the shared individual and collective experiences and references. Furthermore, the framework serves as the limit of our collective understanding and will expand as people learn and share intrapersonal and interpersonal experiences.

The current models of emotional intelligence are points on a continuum, and we might find vestiges of the idea wherever we begin in history. Sun Tzu's The Art of War, Machiavelli's The Prince, and Adam Smith's Theory of Moral Sentiments are three of my favorite markers in the emotional intelligence literature and discussion. What we understand and measure, and our conclusions and future directions will evolve out of the principles we uphold and the values we practice in our social and professional exchanges.

In Homo sapiens thoughts precede behavior, behavior informs habits, habits create a character, and from the creative imagination and the character of the collective arises the concepts and norms of societies. Therefore, intelligence is as fluid as the history of humanity. Stephen Covey's 7 Habits of Highly Effective People is an ideal starting point for understanding and developing valid measures of emotional intelligence.

Sources:

American Psychological Association (APA).
    https://www.apa.org/topics/intelligence/

Armstrong. (n.d.). Multiple Intelligences. *American Institute for Learning and Human Development.* Retrieved from
    http://www.institute4learning.com/resources/articles/multiple-intelligences/

Bar-On, R. (1997). The Emotional Quotient Inventory (EQ-i): A Test of Emotional Intelligence. Toronto, Canada: Multi-Health Systems.

Cherry, K. (2019). Gardner's Theory of Multiple Intelligences. Retrieved from https://www.verywellmind.com/gardners-theory-of-multiple-intelligences-2795161

Gardner, H. (2006). Multiple Intelligences: New Horizons in Theory and Practice. New York: Basic Books.

Gardner, H. (2011). Frames of mind: The theory of multiple intelligences. New York, NY: Basic Books.

Mallery, B. (n.d.). What is emotional intelligence? 2 theories and measures. *Positive Psychology.* Retrieved from
    http://positivepsychology.org.uk/emotional-intelligence-mayer-salovey-theory/

Mayer, J.D., & Salovey, P. (1997). What is emotional intelligence? In P. Salovey & D. Sluyter (eds.), Emotional development and emotional intelligence: Educational Implications (pp.3-31). New York, NY: Perseus Book Group.

Salovey, P., & Mayer, J. D. (1990). Emotional intelligence. Imagination, Cognition, and Personality, 9, 185–211. doi:10.2190/DUGG-P24E-52WK-6CDG

Thiel, E. V. (2019). What is IQ? What is intelligence? 123 Test. Retrieved from https://www.123test.com/what-is-iq-what-is-intelligence/

Thorndike, E. L. (1920). Intelligence and its uses. Harpers Monthly, 227-235. Retrieved from http://harpers.org

Wechsler, D. (1943). Non-intellective factors in general intelligence. The Journal of Abnormal and Social Psychology, 38, 101–103. doi:10.1037/h0060613

ABOUT THE AUTHOR

Dr. Dennis V. Burke is a scholar-practitioner who studies emotional intelligence and managerial effectiveness. He has over 30 years of management experience in the QSR industry, where he is a management and leadership coach. He earned a BS in Workforce Education and Development, MBA with an emphasis in management, and a DBA with an emphasis in finance.

Dr. Burke is an avid student of managerial psychology who studies the role of emotions in decision-making and personal effectiveness. He was born in Jamaica, West Indies, and lives in Florence, South Carolina. He is an educator who teaches that the purpose of education is to create a valid framework for interpreting and understanding our experiences and to serve as the basis in responsible decision-making. He teaches that success begins in the brain.